BEST 100 RECIPES

A Variety of Must-Have Recipes When You Need a Quick Idea

Copyright © 2023 by OffBeat Publishing, LLC

ISBN Paperback: 978-1-950464-31-9

ISBN eBook: 978-1-950464-32-6

All rights reserved.

No portion of this book may be reproduced in any form without written permission from the publisher (OffBeatReads@pm.me), except as permitted by U.S. copyright law.

*Sharing with friends is allowed and encouraged.

For more Titles and More Information Visit: OffBeatReads.com

www.OffBeatReads.com

A Word From the Publisher

Anything that encourages families and friends to get together in a civil way over things they have in common is a good thing. Because food is oftentimes the center of socializing, we felt the desire to compile this book.

From soups to casseroles to desserts, in your hand is a quick reference for a variety of recipes. You'll notice that we have grouped recipes into sections such as, *Breakfasts, Desserts, Hors d'oeuvres, and Appetizers. (Hors d'oeuvres and Appetizers are often referred to as one and the same, but are not. Small offerings frequently served with cocktails before dinner are Hors d'oeuvres; an Appetizer is the first course given while seated at the table to whet the appetite.)* We even thought to give you two pages at the end of each section for recipes you might find elsewhere and want to keep written down where you can find them.

Whether you are learning to cook, looking for a new dish, or needing a quick idea — it is our hope that this collection becomes a trusty tool in aiding you.

Contents

1. Hors d'oeuvres — 1
2. Appetizers — 9
3. Chili — 17
4. Artisan Bread — 25
5. Spaghetti — 33
6. Hamburgers — 42
7. Casseroles — 50
8. Easy Breakfasts — 60
9. Fish — 68
10. Crockpot — 76
11. Lasagna — 84
12. Simple Desserts — 95
13. Punches — 110
14. Simple to Make Candies — 115
15. Breakfasts That Are More Involved — 122
16. Coffee! — 130
17. Potatoes — 135
18. Gravy — 141

19. Pizza 147

Hors d'oeuvres

Deviled Eggs

Ingredients:

6 large eggs

2 tablespoons mayonnaise

1 teaspoon Dijon mustard

1/4 teaspoon salt

Paprika, for garnish

Instructions:

Place the eggs in a saucepan and cover them with cold water. Place the saucepan over high heat and bring the water to a boil. As soon as the water reaches a boil, remove the saucepan from the heat and cover it with a lid. Let the eggs sit in the hot water for 10-12 minutes.

Drain the eggs and place them in a bowl of ice water. Let the eggs cool for a few minutes before peeling them.

Cut the eggs in half lengthwise and scoop the yolks into a small bowl. Set the egg whites aside. Mash the yolks with a fork and stir in the mayonnaise, mustard, and salt.

Spoon the yolk mixture into the egg whites. Garnish the eggs with paprika.

Serve the deviled eggs chilled or at room temperature.

Crostini with Ricotta and Honey

Ingredients:

1 baguette, sliced into 1/4-inch rounds

Olive oil, for brushing

8 ounces ricotta cheese

Honey, for drizzling

Chopped fresh herbs (such as basil or chives), for garnish

Instructions:

Preheat your oven to 400°F (200°C). Line a baking sheet with parchment paper.

Brush both sides of the baguette rounds with olive oil. Arrange the rounds on the prepared baking sheet.

Bake the crostini for 8-10 minutes, until they are lightly toasted. Remove the crostini from the oven and let them cool for a few minutes.

Spread a spoonful of ricotta cheese on each crostini. Drizzle honey over the cheese. Garnish the crostini with chopped herbs.

Serve the crostini immediately.

Baked Brie with Jam

Ingredients:

1 round of brie cheese

1/4 cup fruit jam (such as raspberry or apricot)

Crackers or sliced baguette, for serving

Instructions:

Preheat your oven to 350°F (180°C). Line a baking sheet with parchment paper.

Place the brie cheese on the prepared baking sheet. Spread the jam over the top of the brie.

Bake the brie for 8-10 minutes, until it is soft and gooey.

Serve the brie immediately, with crackers or sliced baguette on the side.

Stuffed Mushrooms

Ingredients:

12 large mushrooms

2 tablespoons olive oil

1/4 cup minced onions

2 cloves garlic, minced

1/2 cup bread crumbs

1/4 cup grated Parmesan cheese

2 tablespoons chopped fresh parsley

1 large egg, beaten

Salt and pepper, to taste

Instructions:

Preheat your oven to 350°F (180°C). Line a baking sheet with parchment paper.

Remove the stems from the mushrooms and chop them finely.

In a large skillet, heat the olive oil over medium heat. Add the onions and garlic and cook for 2-3 minutes, until the onions are translucent. Add the chopped mushroom stems and cook for an additional 2-3 minutes, until the mushrooms are tender. Remove the skillet from the heat and stir in the bread crumbs, Parmesan cheese, parsley, egg, salt, and pepper.

Fill the mushroom caps with the filling mixture. Arrange the mushrooms on the prepared baking sheet.

Bake the mushrooms for 15-20 minutes, until they are tender and the filling is set.

Serve the stuffed mushrooms warm.

Spiced Nuts

Ingredients:

2 cups mixed nuts (such as almonds, cashews, and pecans)

2 tablespoons unsalted butter, melted

1 tablespoon brown sugar

1 teaspoon chili powder

1/2 teaspoon ground cumin

1/2 teaspoon salt

Instructions:

Preheat your oven to 350°F (180°C). Line a baking sheet with parchment paper.

In a large bowl, toss together the nuts, melted butter, brown sugar, chili powder, cumin, and salt. Spread the nuts in a single layer on the prepared baking sheet.

Bake the nuts for 8-10 minutes, until they are fragrant and lightly toasted. Remove the nuts from the oven and let them cool for a few minutes before serving.

Serve the spiced nuts warm or at room temperature.

My Hors d'oeuvre Recipes

Appetizers

Baked Spinach and Artichoke Dip

Ingredients:

10 ounces frozen spinach, thawed and squeezed dry

1 cup frozen artichoke hearts, thawed and diced

8 ounces cream cheese, softened

1/2 cup mayonnaise

1/2 cup grated Parmesan cheese

1/2 cup shredded mozzarella cheese

1 clove garlic, minced

Salt and pepper, to taste

Tortilla chips or sliced baguette, for serving

Instructions:

Preheat your oven to 350°F (180°C). Grease a 9-inch pie dish.

In a large bowl, mix together the spinach, artichoke hearts, cream cheese, mayonnaise, Parmesan cheese, mozzarella cheese, garlic, salt, and pepper. Spread the mixture evenly in the prepared pie dish.

Bake the dip for 25-30 minutes, until it is hot and bubbly.

Serve the dip warm, with tortilla chips or sliced baguette on the side.

Grilled Shrimp Skewers

Ingredients:

1 pound large shrimp, peeled and deveined

1/4 cup olive oil

2 cloves garlic, minced

1 teaspoon paprika

1/2 teaspoon salt

1/4 teaspoon black pepper

Instructions:

Preheat your grill to medium-high heat.

In a small bowl, whisk together the olive oil, garlic, paprika, salt, and pepper. Place the shrimp in a large resealable plastic bag and pour the marinade over the top. Seal the bag and toss the shrimp until they are evenly coated in the marinade.

Thread the shrimp onto skewers. Grill the skewers for 2-3 minutes per side, until the shrimp are pink and opaque.

Serve the grilled shrimp skewers immediately.

Sausage and Pepper Skewers

Ingredients:

1 pound Italian sausage, cut into 1-inch pieces

1 red bell pepper, cut into 1-inch pieces

1 green bell pepper, cut into 1-inch pieces

1 yellow bell pepper, cut into 1-inch pieces

1/4 cup olive oil

2 cloves garlic, minced

1 teaspoon dried oregano

1/2 teaspoon salt

1/4 teaspoon black pepper

Instructions:

Preheat your grill to medium-high heat.

Thread the sausage, red pepper, green pepper, and yellow pepper onto skewers. In a small bowl, whisk together the olive oil, garlic, oregano, salt, and pepper. Brush the skewers with the marinade.

Grill the skewers for 8-10 minutes, turning them occasionally, until the sausage is cooked through and the vegetables are tender.

Serve the sausage and pepper skewers immediately.

Buffalo Chicken Dip

Ingredients:

2 cups shredded cooked chicken

8 ounces cream cheese, softened

1/2 cup Frank's RedHot sauce

1/2 cup ranch dressing

1/2 cup shredded mozzarella cheese

Celery sticks or carrot sticks, for serving

Instructions:

Preheat your oven to 350°F (180°C). Grease a 9-inch pie dish.

In a large bowl, mix together the chicken, cream cheese, RedHot sauce, ranch dressing, and mozzarella cheese. Spread the mixture evenly in the prepared pie dish.

Bake the dip for 20-25 minutes, until it is hot and bubbly.

Serve the dip warm, with celery or carrot sticks on the side.

Caprese Skewers

Ingredients:

1 pint cherry tomatoes

1 ball fresh mozzarella, cut into 1-inch cubes

Fresh basil leaves

1/4 cup olive oil

2 tablespoons balsamic vinegar

Salt and pepper, to taste

Instructions:

Thread the cherry tomatoes, mozzarella cubes, and basil leaves onto skewers, alternating the ingredients.

In a small bowl, whisk together the olive oil, balsamic vinegar, salt, and pepper. Brush the skewers with the marinade.

Serve the caprese skewers immediately.

My Appetizers

Chili

Classic Beef Chili

Ingredients:

1 pound ground beef

1 medium onion, chopped

1 green bell pepper, chopped

1 garlic clove, minced

1 can (14-1/2 ounces) diced tomatoes, undrained

1 can (8 ounces) tomato sauce

1 can (6 ounces) tomato paste

1 can (4 ounces) chopped green chilies

1 tablespoon chili powder

1 teaspoon ground cumin

1/2 teaspoon salt

1/4 teaspoon pepper

1 can (15-1/2 ounces) kidney beans, rinsed and drained

Instructions:

In a large saucepan, cook beef, onion, bell pepper, and garlic over medium heat until meat is no longer pink; drain.

Stir in the tomatoes, tomato sauce, tomato paste, chilies, chili powder, cumin, salt, and pepper. Bring to a boil.

Reduce heat; simmer, uncovered, for 1 hour.

Stir in beans. Simmer for 15-20 minutes longer or until heated through.

Slow Cooker Chicken Chili

Ingredients:

1 pound boneless, skinless chicken breasts

1 medium onion, chopped

1 red bell pepper, chopped

1 jalapeno pepper, seeded and minced

1 garlic clove, minced

1 can (14-1/2 ounces) diced tomatoes, undrained

1 can (15 ounces) black beans, rinsed and drained

1 can (11 ounces) corn, drained

1 can (4 ounces) diced green chilies

1 tablespoon chili powder

1 teaspoon ground cumin

1/2 teaspoon salt

1/4 teaspoon pepper

1/4 cup minced fresh cilantro

Instructions:

In a 5-qt. slow cooker, combine the first 13 ingredients. Cover and cook on low for 6-8 hours or until the chicken is tender.

Stir in cilantro. Cover and cook for 15 minutes longer.

Vegetarian Chili

Ingredients:

1 medium onion, chopped

1 green bell pepper, chopped

1 red bell pepper, chopped

1 cup chopped fresh mushrooms

1 garlic clove, minced

1 can (14-1/2 ounces) diced tomatoes, undrained

1 can (15 ounces) kidney beans, rinsed and drained

1 can (15 ounces) black beans, rinsed and drained

1 can (14-1/2 ounces) tomato sauce

1 can (6 ounces) tomato paste

1/2 cup water

2 tablespoons chili powder

1 tablespoon ground cumin

1 teaspoon dried oregano

1/2 teaspoon salt

1/4 teaspoon pepper

Instructions:

In a large saucepan, cook the onion, peppers, mushrooms, and garlic over medium heat until tender.

Stir in the remaining ingredients. Bring to a boil.

Reduce heat; simmer, uncovered, for 1 hour.

Slow Cooker BBQ Beef Chili

Ingredients:

1 pound beef stew meat, cut into 1-inch cubes

1 medium onion, chopped

1 can (14-1/2 ounces) diced tomatoes, undrained

1 can (6 ounces) tomato paste

1/2 cup barbecue sauce

1/2 cup beef broth

2 tablespoons chili powder

1 tablespoon Worcestershire sauce

1 garlic clove, minced

1 teaspoon ground cumin

1/2 teaspoon salt

1/4 teaspoon pepper

1 can (15-1/2 ounces) kidney beans, rinsed and drained

Instructions:

In a 3-qt. slow cooker, combine the first 12 ingredients. Cover and cook on low for 6-8 hours or until the beef is tender.

Stir in beans. Cover and cook for 15 minutes longer or until heated through.

Three-Bean Chili

Ingredients:

1 medium onion, chopped

1 green bell pepper, chopped

1 garlic clove, minced

1 tablespoon olive oil

1 pound ground beef

1 can (14-1/2 ounces) diced tomatoes, undrained

1 can (8 ounces) tomato sauce

1 can (6 ounces) tomato paste

1 can (4 ounces) chopped green chilies

1 tablespoon chili powder

1 teaspoon ground cumin

1/2 teaspoon salt

1/4 teaspoon pepper

1 can (15 ounces) kidney beans, rinsed and drained

1 can (15 ounces) black beans, rinsed and drained

1 can (15-1/4 ounces) whole kernel corn, drained

Instructions:

In a large saucepan, saute the onion, bell pepper, and garlic in oil until tender. Add beef; cook until meat is no longer pink.

Stir in the tomatoes, tomato sauce, tomato paste, chilies, chili powder, cumin, salt, and pepper. Bring to a boil.

Reduce heat; simmer, uncovered, for 1 hour.

Stir in beans and corn. Simmer for 15-20 minutes longer or until heated through.

My Chili Recipes

Artisan Bread

No-Knead Artisan Bread

Ingredients:

3 cups all-purpose flour

1-1/2 teaspoons salt

1/4 teaspoon instant yeast

1-1/2 cups water

Instructions:

In a large bowl, mix together the flour, salt, and yeast. Add the water and stir until a shaggy dough forms.

Cover the bowl with plastic wrap and let the dough rest at room temperature for 8-24 hours.

Preheat your oven to 450°F (230°C). Place a Dutch oven or other heavy pot with a lid in the oven as it preheats.

Once the oven and pot are preheated, carefully remove the pot from the oven and place the dough inside. Cover the pot and return it to the oven.

Bake the bread for 30 minutes, then remove the lid and continue baking for another 15-30 minutes, until the bread is a deep golden brown.

Remove the bread from the pot and let it cool on a wire rack.

Sourdough Bread

Ingredients:

1 cup sourdough starter

2-1/2 cups all-purpose flour

1 teaspoon salt

Instructions:

In a large bowl, mix together the sourdough starter, flour, and salt until a shaggy dough forms.

Transfer the dough to a lightly floured surface and knead for about 10 minutes, until it becomes smooth and elastic.

Place the dough in a lightly greased bowl, cover with a damp cloth, and let it rise in a warm place for 8-12 hours.

Preheat your oven to 450°F (230°C).

Shape the dough into a round loaf and place it on a baking sheet lined with parchment paper. Use a sharp knife to make a few shallow slashes across the top of the loaf.

Bake the bread for 30-35 minutes, until it is golden brown and sounds hollow when tapped.

Remove the bread from the oven and let it cool on a wire rack.

Ciabatta Bread

Ingredients:

1-3/4 cups water, at room temperature

1 tablespoon honey

2-1/4 teaspoons active dry yeast (1 packet)

4 cups all-purpose flour

1 tablespoon salt

Instructions:

In a small bowl, combine the water, honey, and yeast. Let the mixture sit for 5-10 minutes, until the yeast becomes frothy.

In a large bowl, mix together the flour and salt. Add the yeast mixture and stir until a sticky dough forms.

Transfer the dough to a lightly floured surface and knead for about 10 minutes, until it becomes smooth and elastic.

Place the dough in a lightly greased bowl, cover with a damp cloth, and let it rise in a warm place for 1-2 hours, until it has doubled in size.

Preheat your oven to 450°F (230°C).

Divide the dough into two equal pieces and shape each piece into a long, narrow loaf. Place the loaves on a baking sheet lined with parchment paper.

Bake the bread for 20-25 minutes, until it is golden brown and sounds hollow when tapped.

Remove the bread from the oven and let it cool on a wire rack.

Focaccia Bread

Ingredients:

4-1/2 cups all-purpose flour

1 tablespoon sugar

2-1/4 teaspoons active dry yeast (1 packet)

1-1/2 teaspoons salt

1-3/4 cups water, at room temperature

3 tablespoons olive oil, plus more for drizzling

coarse salt and herbs for topping (optional)

Instructions:

In a large bowl, mix together the flour, sugar, yeast, and salt. Add the water and 3 tablespoons of olive oil, and stir until a soft dough forms.

Transfer the dough to a lightly floured surface and knead for about 10 minutes, until it becomes smooth and elastic.

Place the dough in a lightly greased bowl, cover with a damp cloth, and let it rise in a warm place for 1-2 hours, until it has doubled in size.

Preheat your oven to 425°F (220°C).

Press the dough into a large, greased baking sheet, stretching it to fit the pan. Use your fingertips to make dimples all over the surface of the dough.

Drizzle the dough with a little bit of olive oil and sprinkle with coarse salt and herbs, if desired.

Bake the bread for 20-25 minutes, until it is golden brown and sounds hollow when tapped.

Remove the bread from the oven and let it cool on a wire rack.

Rosemary Sea Salt Focaccia

Ingredients:

4-1/2 cups all-purpose flour

1 tablespoon sugar

2-1/4 teaspoons active dry yeast (1 packet)

1-1/2 teaspoons salt

1-3/4 cups water, at room temperature

3 tablespoons olive oil, plus more for drizzling

2 tablespoons chopped fresh rosemary

1 teaspoon coarse sea salt

Instructions:

In a large bowl, mix together the flour, sugar, yeast, and salt. Add the water and 3 tablespoons of olive oil, and stir until a soft dough forms.

Transfer the dough to a lightly floured surface and knead for about 10 minutes, until it becomes smooth and elastic.

Place the dough in a lightly greased bowl, cover with a damp cloth, and let it rise in a warm place for 1-2 hours, until it has doubled in size.

Preheat your oven to 425°F (220°C).

Press the dough into a large, greased baking sheet, stretching it to fit the pan. Use your fingertips to make dimples all over the surface of the dough.

Drizzle the dough with a little bit of olive oil and sprinkle with the chopped rosemary and coarse sea salt.

Bake the bread for 20-25 minutes, until it is golden brown and sounds hollow when tapped.

Remove the bread from the oven and let it cool on a wire rack.

My Artisan Bread Recipes

Spaghetti

Classic Spaghetti and Meatballs

Ingredients:

1 pound ground beef

1 egg, beaten

1/4 cup bread crumbs

1/4 cup grated Parmesan cheese

1 garlic clove, minced

1/2 teaspoon salt

1/4 teaspoon pepper

1 tablespoon olive oil

1 large onion, diced

2 cloves garlic, minced

1 can (28 ounces) crushed tomatoes

1 can (6 ounces) tomato paste

1 teaspoon dried basil

1 teaspoon dried oregano

1/2 teaspoon salt

1/4 teaspoon pepper

1 pound spaghetti

Fresh parsley, for garnish

Instructions:

Preheat your oven to 400°F (200°C).

In a large bowl, mix together the ground beef, egg, bread crumbs, Parmesan cheese, minced garlic, salt, and pepper. Shape the mixture into 1-inch balls and place them on a baking sheet.

Bake the meatballs for 20-25 minutes, until they are browned and cooked through.

While the meatballs are baking, heat the olive oil in a large saucepan over medium heat. Add the diced onion and minced garlic and cook until the onion is translucent.

Continued...

Stir in the crushed tomatoes, tomato paste, basil, oregano, salt, and pepper. Bring the sauce to a simmer and let it cook for about 10 minutes, until it has thickened slightly.

Add the cooked meatballs to the sauce and let them simmer for about 5 minutes, until they are heated through.

Meanwhile, bring a large pot of salted water to a boil. Add the spaghetti and cook according to the package directions.

Drain the spaghetti and transfer it to a large serving bowl. Top the spaghetti with the meatballs and sauce, and garnish with fresh parsley.

Spaghetti Carbonara

Ingredients:

1 pound spaghetti

4 eggs

1 cup grated Parmesan cheese

1/2 cup pancetta or bacon, diced

2 cloves garlic, minced

2 tablespoons chopped fresh parsley

Salt and pepper, to taste

Instructions:

Bring a large pot of salted water to a boil. Add the spaghetti and cook according to the package directions.

While the spaghetti is cooking, whisk together the eggs, Parmesan cheese, and a pinch of salt and pepper in a small bowl. Set aside.

In a large skillet, cook the pancetta over medium heat until it is crispy. Add the minced garlic and cook for another minute, until the garlic is fragrant.

Drain the spaghetti and add it to the skillet with the pancetta. Pour the egg mixture over the top and toss everything together until the spaghetti is coated with the sauce.

Serve the spaghetti carbonara hot, garnished with chopped fresh parsley.

Spaghetti Bolognese

Ingredients:

1 tablespoon olive oil

1 small onion, diced

2 cloves garlic, minced

1 pound ground beef

1 can (14.5 ounces) diced tomatoes

1 can (6 ounces) tomato paste

1 cup beef broth

1 teaspoon dried basil

1 teaspoon dried oregano

Salt and pepper to taste

1 pound spaghetti

Grated Parmesan cheese, for serving

Instructions:

Heat the olive oil in a large saucepan over medium heat. Add the onion and garlic and cook until the onion is translucent, about 5 minutes.

Add the ground beef to the pan and cook until it is browned, about 5 minutes more.

Stir in the diced tomatoes, tomato paste, beef broth, basil, oregano, salt, and pepper. Reduce the heat to low and simmer for 20 minutes.

While the sauce is simmering, bring a large pot of salted water to a boil. Add the spaghetti and cook according to the package instructions until it is al dente.

Drain the spaghetti and divide it among serving bowls. Top each serving with the bolognese sauce and a sprinkle of Parmesan cheese.

Spaghetti with Garlic and Olive Oil

Ingredients:

1 pound spaghetti

1/4 cup olive oil

4 cloves garlic, minced

1/4 teaspoon red pepper flakes (optional)

Salt and pepper, to taste

Grated Parmesan cheese, for serving

Instructions:

Bring a large pot of salted water to a boil. Add the spaghetti and cook according to the package directions.

While the spaghetti is cooking, heat the olive oil in a large skillet over medium heat. Add the minced garlic and red pepper flakes (if using) and cook until the garlic is fragrant.

Drain the spaghetti and add it to the skillet with the garlic and olive oil. Toss everything together until the spaghetti is coated with the sauce.

Serve the spaghetti hot, garnished with grated Parmesan cheese.

Spaghetti with Meat Sauce

Ingredients:

1 pound spaghetti

1 tablespoon olive oil

1 medium onion, diced

1 pound ground beef

1 can (14-1/2 ounces) diced tomatoes, undrained

1 can (6 ounces) tomato paste

1 cup beef broth

1 tablespoon Worcestershire sauce

1 teaspoon dried basil

1 teaspoon dried oregano

1/2 teaspoon salt

1/4 teaspoon pepper

Grated Parmesan cheese, for serving

Instructions:

Bring a large pot of salted water to a boil. Add the spaghetti and cook according to the package directions.

While the spaghetti is cooking, heat the olive oil in a large skillet over medium heat. Add the diced onion and cook until it is translucent.

Add the ground beef to the skillet and cook until it is browned. Drain any excess fat.

Stir in the diced tomatoes, tomato paste, beef broth, Worcestershire sauce, basil, oregano, salt, and pepper. Bring the sauce to a simmer and let it cook for about 10 minutes, until it has thickened slightly.

Drain the spaghetti and transfer it to a large serving bowl. Top the spaghetti with the meat sauce and garnish with grated Parmesan cheese.

My Spaghetti Recipes

Hamburgers

Classic Hamburger

Ingredients:

1 pound ground beef

4 hamburger buns

Lettuce, tomato, onion, and pickles, for serving

Ketchup, mustard, and mayonnaise, for serving

Instructions:

Preheat your grill or stovetop grill pan to medium-high heat.

Divide the ground beef into four equal portions and shape each portion into a patty. Make a small indentation in the center of each patty to prevent it from puffing up as it cooks.

Place the patties on the grill and cook for about 4-5 minutes per side, until they are cooked to your desired level of doneness.

Assemble the hamburgers by placing a patty on the bottom half of each bun. Top the patties with lettuce, tomato, onion, and pickles, and add a dollop of ketchup, mustard, and mayonnaise. Cover each hamburger with the top half of the bun and serve.

Mushroom and Swiss Hamburger

Ingredients:

1 pound ground beef

4 hamburger buns

4 slices Swiss cheese

1 cup sliced mushrooms

2 tablespoons butter

Lettuce, tomato, onion, and pickles, for serving

Ketchup, mustard, and mayonnaise, for serving

Instructions:

Preheat your grill or stovetop grill pan to medium-high heat.

Divide the ground beef into four equal portions and shape each portion into a patty. Make a small indentation in the center of each patty to prevent it from puffing up as it cooks.

Place the patties on the grill and cook for about 4-5 minutes per side, until they are cooked to your desired level of doneness.

While the patties are cooking, melt the butter in a small skillet over medium heat. Add the sliced mushrooms and cook until they are tender.

Assemble the hamburgers by placing a patty on the bottom half of each bun. Top the patties with a slice of Swiss cheese, a handful of cooked mushrooms, and lettuce, tomato, onion, and pickles. Add a dollop of ketchup, mustard, and mayonnaise, and cover each hamburger with the top half of the bun.

BBQ Bacon Cheeseburger

Ingredients:

1 pound ground beef

4 hamburger buns

4 slices cheddar cheese

4 slices bacon, cooked

1/2 cup BBQ sauce

Lettuce, tomato, onion, and pickles, for serving

Instructions:

Preheat your grill or stovetop grill pan to medium-high heat.

Divide the ground beef into four equal portions and shape each portion into a patty. Make a small indentation in the center of each patty to prevent it from puffing up as it cooks.

Place the patties on the grill and cook for about 4-5 minutes per side, until they are cooked to your desired level of doneness.

Assemble the hamburgers by placing a patty on the bottom half of each bun. Top the patties with a slice of cheddar cheese, two slices of bacon, and a generous drizzle of BBQ sauce. Add lettuce, tomato, onion, and pickles, and cover each hamburger with the top half of the bun.

Jalapeno Popper Burger

Ingredients:

1 pound ground beef

4 jalapeno peppers, sliced

4 ounces cream cheese, softened

1/2 cup shredded cheddar cheese

4 hamburger buns

Lettuce, tomato, and other desired toppings

Instructions:

Preheat your grill to medium-high heat.

In a medium bowl, mix together the cream cheese and cheddar cheese.

Divide the ground beef into 4 equal portions and shape each portion into a patty. Make a small indentation in the center of each patty.

Divide the cheese mixture into 4 equal portions and place a portion in the indentation of each patty. Top the cheese with jalapeno slices.

Carefully place the patties on the grill and cook for 4-6 minutes per side, or until they reach your desired level of doneness.

Toast the hamburger buns on the grill for a minute or two, until they are lightly golden.

Assemble the burgers by placing a patty on each bun, followed by lettuce, tomato, and any other desired toppings. Serve immediately.

Black Bean Burger

Ingredients:

1 can (15 ounces) black beans, drained and rinsed

1/2 cup bread crumbs

1/4 cup grated cheddar cheese

1 egg, beaten

1 jalapeno pepper, seeded and minced

1/2 teaspoon cumin

1/2 teaspoon chili powder

4 hamburger buns

Lettuce, tomato, onion, and pickles, for serving

Ketchup, mustard, and mayonnaise, for serving

Instructions:

Preheat your grill or stovetop grill pan to medium-high heat.

In a large bowl, mash the black beans with a fork or potato masher until they are mostly smooth. Stir in the bread crumbs, cheddar cheese, egg, minced jalapeno pepper, cumin, and chili powder.

Divide the mixture into four equal portions and shape each portion into a patty. Place the patties on the grill and cook for about 4-5 minutes per side, until they are heated through and slightly crispy on the outside.

Assemble the hamburgers by placing a patty on the bottom half of each bun. Add lettuce, tomato, onion, and pickles, and add a dollop of ketchup, mustard, and mayonnaise. Cover each hamburger with the top half of the bun and serve.

My Hamburger Recipes

Casseroles

Chicken and Rice Casserole

Ingredients:

1 pound boneless, skinless chicken breasts, cut into bite-sized pieces

1 cup uncooked white rice

1 can (10-3/4 ounces) cream of chicken soup

1 can (10-3/4 ounces) cream of mushroom soup

1 cup chicken broth

1/2 cup milk

1/2 cup grated Parmesan cheese

1/2 teaspoon garlic powder

1/2 teaspoon onion powder

1/2 teaspoon paprika

1/2 teaspoon salt

1/4 teaspoon pepper

2 cups frozen broccoli florets

2 cups shredded cheddar cheese

Instructions:

Preheat your oven to 350°F (180°C).

In a large saucepan, bring the chicken broth to a boil. Add the rice and stir to combine. Reduce the heat to low, cover the saucepan, and let the rice simmer for about 18-20 minutes, until it is tender.

Meanwhile, heat a large skillet over medium heat. Add the chicken pieces and cook until they are no longer pink.

In a large bowl, whisk together the cream of chicken soup, cream of mushroom soup, milk, Parmesan cheese, garlic powder, onion powder, paprika, salt, and pepper.

Stir the cooked chicken and rice into the soup mixture. Add the frozen broccoli and mix everything together until it is well combined.

Continued...

Pour the mixture into a large, greased casserole dish. Sprinkle the shredded cheddar cheese over the top.

Cover the dish with foil and bake the casserole for 30 minutes. Remove the foil and bake for an additional 10-15 minutes, until the casserole is hot and the cheese is melted and bubbly.

Beef and Noodle Casserole

Ingredients:

1 pound ground beef

1 medium onion, diced

2 cloves garlic, minced

1 can (14-1/2 ounces) diced tomatoes, undrained

1 can (8 ounces) tomato sauce

1 teaspoon dried basil

1 teaspoon dried oregano

1/2 teaspoon salt

1/4 teaspoon pepper

8 ounces wide egg noodles

1 cup sour cream

1 cup grated cheddar cheese

Instructions:

Preheat your oven to 350°F (180°C).

In a large skillet, cook the ground beef over medium heat until it is browned. Add the diced onion and minced garlic and cook until the onion is translucent.

Stir in the diced tomatoes, tomato sauce, basil, oregano, salt, and pepper. Bring the mixture to a simmer and let it cook for about 10 minutes, until it has thickened slightly.

Meanwhile, cook the egg noodles according to the package directions. Drain the noodles and add them to the skillet with the beef mixture. Stir in the sour cream and mix everything together until it is well combined.

Pour the mixture into a large, greased casserole dish. Sprinkle the grated cheddar cheese over the top.

Bake the casserole for 25-30 minutes, until it is hot and the cheese is melted and bubbly.

Tuna Noodle Casserole

Ingredients:

8 ounces egg noodles

2 tablespoons butter

2 tablespoons all-purpose flour

1 cup milk

1 cup chicken broth

1 cup shredded Cheddar cheese

1/2 cup frozen peas

2 cans (5 ounces each) tuna, drained and flaked

1/2 cup crushed crackers

2 tablespoons melted butter

Instructions:

Preheat your oven to 350°F (180°C).

Bring a large pot of salted water to a boil and cook the noodles according to the package instructions until they are al dente. Drain the noodles and set them aside.

In a medium saucepan, melt the butter over medium heat. Add the flour and cook, stirring constantly, for 1 minute.

Gradually add the milk and chicken broth, whisking constantly, until the mixture is smooth. Bring the sauce to a boil and cook until it has thickened, about 2 minutes.

Remove the saucepan from the heat and stir in the cheese, peas, and tuna. Add the noodles to the sauce and stir until they are evenly coated.

Transfer the mixture to a 9x13-inch baking dish. In a small bowl, mix together the crushed crackers and melted butter. Sprinkle the crumb mixture over the top of the casserole.

Bake the casserole for 20-25 minutes, or until it is hot and bubbly. Serve immediately.

Chili Mac Casserole

Ingredients:

1 pound ground beef

1 medium onion, diced

2 cloves garlic, minced

1 can (14-1/2 ounces) diced tomatoes, undrained

1 can (8 ounces) tomato sauce

1 can (4 ounces) diced green chilies

1 tablespoon chili powder

1 teaspoon cumin

1/2 teaspoon salt

1/4 teaspoon pepper

8 ounces elbow macaroni

1 cup grated cheddar cheese

Instructions:

Preheat your oven to 350°F (180°C).

Continued...

In a large skillet, cook the ground beef over medium heat until it is browned. Add the diced onion and minced garlic and cook until the onion is translucent.

Stir in the diced tomatoes, tomato sauce, diced green chilies, chili powder, cumin, salt, and pepper. Bring the mixture to a simmer and let it cook for about 10 minutes, until it has thickened slightly.

Meanwhile, cook the elbow macaroni according to the package directions. Drain the macaroni and add it to the skillet with the beef mixture. Mix everything together until it is well combined.

Pour the mixture into a large, greased casserole dish. Sprinkle the grated cheddar cheese over the top.

Bake the casserole for 25-30 minutes, until it is hot and the cheese is melted and bubbly.

Chicken Pot Pie Casserole

Ingredients:

2 cups cooked, diced chicken

1 can (10-3/4 ounces) cream of chicken soup

1 can (10-3/4 ounces) cream of mushroom soup

1 cup frozen peas and carrots

1/2 cup milk

1/2 teaspoon salt

1/4 teaspoon pepper

2 cups biscuit mix

1/2 cup milk

1/4 cup butter, melted

Instructions:

Preheat your oven to 350°F (180°C).

In a large bowl, mix together the cooked chicken, cream of chicken soup, cream of mushroom soup, frozen peas and carrots, milk, salt, and pepper. Spread the mixture into a large, greased casserole dish.

In a medium bowl, stir together the biscuit mix and milk until a soft dough forms. Drop the dough by spoonfuls on top of the chicken mixture.

Brush the top of the biscuit dough with melted butter.

Bake the casserole for 30-35 minutes, until the biscuit topping is golden brown and the filling is hot and bubbly.

My Casserole Recipes

Easy Breakfasts

Scrambled Eggs

Ingredients:

4 eggs

2 tablespoons milk

Salt and pepper, to taste

1 tablespoon butter

Instructions:

In a small bowl, beat together the eggs, milk, salt, and pepper.

Heat a small skillet over medium heat. Add the butter and let it melt.

Pour the egg mixture into the skillet and let it cook for about 1-2 minutes, until the bottom starts to set. Use a spatula to gently stir the eggs, scraping the bottom and sides of the skillet as you go.

Continue cooking the eggs until they are set to your desired level of doneness. Serve the scrambled eggs hot.

French Toast

Ingredients:

4 slices bread

2 eggs

1/2 cup milk

1/2 teaspoon vanilla extract

1/4 teaspoon cinnamon

Butter, for cooking

Instructions:

In a shallow dish, whisk together the eggs, milk, vanilla extract, and cinnamon.

Dip each slice of bread into the egg mixture, making sure to coat both sides.

Heat a large skillet over medium heat. Add a pat of butter and let it melt.

Place the bread slices in the skillet and cook for about 2-3 minutes per side, until they are golden brown.

Serve the French toast hot, topped with your favorite toppings such as syrup, powdered sugar, fruit, or whipped cream.

Pancakes

Ingredients:

1 cup all-purpose flour

2 tablespoons sugar

1 teaspoon baking powder

1/2 teaspoon baking soda

1/2 teaspoon salt

1 cup milk

1 egg

2 tablespoons melted butter

Instructions:

In a medium bowl, whisk together the flour, sugar, baking powder, baking soda, and salt.

In a small bowl, beat together the milk, egg, and melted butter.

Pour the wet ingredients into the dry ingredients and stir until a smooth batter forms.

Heat a large skillet or griddle over medium heat. Drop spoonfuls of the pancake batter onto the skillet, using about 1/4 cup of batter per pancake.

Cook the pancakes for about 2-3 minutes per side, until they are golden brown and cooked through. Serve the pancakes hot, topped with your favorite toppings such as syrup, fruit, or whipped cream.

Omelette

Ingredients:

3 eggs

2 tablespoons milk

Salt and pepper, to taste

1/4 cup diced ham

1/4 cup diced bell pepper

1/4 cup grated cheese

1 tablespoon butter

Instructions:

In a small bowl, beat together the eggs, milk, salt, and pepper.

Heat a small skillet over medium heat. Add the butter and let it melt.

Pour the egg mixture into the skillet and let it cook for about 1-2 minutes, until the bottom starts to set.

Sprinkle the ham, bell pepper, and grated cheese over one half of the omelette. Use a spatula to gently fold the other half of the omelette over the filling.

Continue cooking the omelette for about 1-2 minutes, until it is set to your desired level of doneness. Serve the omelette hot.

Breakfast Burrito

Ingredients:

4 eggs

1/4 cup diced onion

1/4 cup diced bell pepper

1/4 cup diced tomato

1/4 cup diced ham

4 tortillas

1/4 cup grated cheese

Salsa and sour cream, for serving (optional)

Instructions:

Heat a large skillet over medium heat. Add the eggs and let them cook for about 1-2 minutes, until the bottom starts to set. Use a spatula to gently stir the eggs, scraping the bottom and sides of the skillet as you go.

When the eggs are almost cooked to your desired level of doneness, add the diced onion, bell pepper, tomato, and ham to the skillet. Stir everything together and cook for about 1-2 minutes, until the vegetables are tender and the eggs are fully cooked.

Divide the egg mixture evenly among the tortillas, placing it in the center of each tortilla. Sprinkle a tablespoon of grated cheese over the top of the egg mixture.

Fold the sides of the tortillas over the filling, then roll up the tortillas burrito-style.

Serve the breakfast burritos hot, with salsa and sour cream on the side if desired.

My Breakfast Recipes

Fish

Grilled Salmon

Ingredients:

4 salmon fillets (about 6 ounces each)

2 tablespoons olive oil

1 tablespoon lemon juice

1 teaspoon garlic powder

1 teaspoon onion powder

1/2 teaspoon salt

1/4 teaspoon black pepper

Instructions:

Preheat your grill to medium-high heat (about 400°F / 200°C).

In a small bowl, whisk together the olive oil, lemon juice, garlic powder, onion powder, salt, and pepper.

Brush the salmon fillets on both sides with the oil mixture.

Place the salmon fillets on the grill and cook for about 6-8 minutes per side, until they are cooked through and flake easily with a fork.

Serve the grilled salmon hot, with your favorite sides.

Baked Cod

Ingredients:

4 cod fillets (about 6 ounces each)

2 tablespoons butter, melted

2 tablespoons lemon juice

1 teaspoon garlic powder

1 teaspoon onion powder

1/2 teaspoon salt

1/4 teaspoon black pepper

1/4 cup breadcrumbs

2 tablespoons grated Parmesan cheese

Instructions:

Preheat your oven to 400°F (200°C).

Place the cod fillets in a large, greased baking dish.

In a small bowl, whisk together the melted butter, lemon juice, garlic powder, onion powder, salt, and pepper. Brush the mixture over the top of the cod fillets.

In a separate small bowl, mix together the breadcrumbs and Parmesan cheese. Sprinkle the breadcrumb mixture over the top of the cod fillets.

Bake the cod for about 15-20 minutes, until it is cooked through and flakes easily with a fork.

Serve the baked cod hot, with your favorite sides.

Pan-Seared Trout

Ingredients:

4 trout fillets (about 6 ounces each)

2 tablespoons olive oil

1 tablespoon lemon juice

1 teaspoon garlic powder

1 teaspoon onion powder

1/2 teaspoon salt

1/4 teaspoon black pepper

Instructions:

Heat a large skillet over medium-high heat. Add the olive oil and let it heat up.

In a small bowl, whisk together the lemon juice, garlic powder, onion powder, salt, and pepper. Brush the mixture over both sides of the trout fillets.

Place the trout fillets in the hot skillet and cook for about 3-4 minutes per side, until they are cooked through and flakes easily with a fork.

Serve the pan-seared trout hot, with your favorite sides.

Poached Salmon

Ingredients:

4 salmon fillets (about 6 ounces each)

2 cups water

2 cups chicken broth

1 carrot, thinly sliced

1 onion, thinly sliced

1 celery stalk, thinly sliced

1 bay leaf

1 teaspoon black peppercorns

1/2 teaspoon salt

Instructions:

Place the salmon fillets in a large, shallow pan. Add the water, chicken broth, carrot, onion, celery, bay leaf, peppercorns, and salt to the pan.

Bring the liquid to a boil over high heat. Reduce the heat to low and let the liquid simmer for about 8-10 minutes, until the salmon is cooked through and flakes easily with a fork.

Use a slotted spoon to remove the salmon fillets from the pan and place them on a plate. Discard the cooking liquid.

Serve the poached salmon hot, with your favorite sides.

Crispy Fried Tilapia

Ingredients:

4 tilapia fillets (about 6 ounces each)

1 cup all-purpose flour

1 teaspoon salt

1/2 teaspoon black pepper

1 cup milk

2 cups panko breadcrumbs

Vegetable oil, for frying

Instructions:

In a shallow dish, mix together the flour, salt, and pepper.

In a separate shallow dish, pour the milk.

In a third shallow dish, pour the panko breadcrumbs.

Dip each tilapia fillet into the flour mixture, coating both sides. Shake off any excess flour. Dip the floured tilapia fillets into the milk, coating both sides. Let any excess milk drip off. Dip the milk-coated tilapia fillets into the panko breadcrumbs, coating both sides.

Heat a large skillet over medium-high heat. Add enough vegetable oil to the skillet to come up the sides by about 1/2 inch. Let the oil heat up until it reaches 375°F (190°C).

Place the breaded tilapia fillets in the hot oil and cook for about 3-4 minutes per side, until they are golden brown and crispy. Use a slotted spoon to transfer the fried tilapia fillets to a plate lined with paper towels to drain any excess oil.

Serve the crispy fried tilapia hot, with your favorite dipping sauces.

My Fish Recipes

Crockpot

Beef Stew

Ingredients:

2 pounds beef stew meat

1 large onion, diced

3 cloves garlic, minced

2 carrots, peeled and sliced

2 potatoes, peeled and diced

1 cup beef broth

1 cup tomato sauce

1 tablespoon Worcestershire sauce

1 teaspoon paprika

1 teaspoon salt

1/2 teaspoon black pepper

Instructions:

Place the beef stew meat, onion, garlic, carrots, potatoes, beef broth, tomato sauce, Worcestershire sauce, paprika, salt, and pepper in a crockpot. Stir everything together.

Cover the crockpot and cook the stew on low heat for 8-10 hours, or on high heat for 4-5 hours, until the beef is tender.

Serve the beef stew hot, with your favorite crusty bread or rolls on the side.

Chicken Noodle Soup

Ingredients:

1 pound boneless, skinless chicken breasts

1 large onion, diced

2 cloves garlic, minced

2 carrots, peeled and sliced

2 celery stalks, sliced

8 cups chicken broth

2 tablespoons chopped fresh parsley

1 teaspoon salt

1/2 teaspoon black pepper

8 ounces egg noodles

Instructions:

Place the chicken breasts, onion, garlic, carrots, celery, chicken broth, parsley, salt, and pepper in a crockpot. Stir everything together.

Cover the crockpot and cook the soup on low heat for 8-10 hours, or on high heat for 4-5 hours, until the chicken is cooked through and tender.

Use a fork to shred the chicken into bite-sized pieces.

Stir the egg noodles into the soup. Cover the crockpot and cook the soup on high heat for an additional 15-20 minutes, until the noodles are cooked through.

Serve the chicken noodle soup hot.

BBQ Pork

Ingredients:

2 pounds pork shoulder roast

1 cup BBQ sauce

1/4 cup brown sugar

2 tablespoons apple cider vinegar

1 tablespoon Worcestershire sauce

1 teaspoon salt

1/2 teaspoon black pepper

1/4 teaspoon garlic powder

Instructions:

Place the pork shoulder roast in a crockpot.

In a small bowl, whisk together the BBQ sauce, brown sugar, apple cider vinegar, Worcestershire sauce, salt, pepper, and garlic powder. Pour the sauce over the pork roast.

Cover the crockpot and cook the pork on low heat for 8-10 hours, or on high heat for 4-5 hours, until it is tender and falls apart easily with a fork.

Use a fork to shred the pork into bite-sized pieces. Stir the pork to coat it evenly with the BBQ sauce.

Serve the BBQ pork hot, with your favorite sides.

Chili

Ingredients:

1 pound ground beef

1 large onion, diced

2 cloves garlic, minced

2 carrots, peeled and diced

2 stalks celery, diced

1 red bell pepper, diced

1 cup beef broth

1 (15-ounce) can kidney beans, drained and rinsed

1 (14.5-ounce) can diced tomatoes

1 (6-ounce) can tomato paste

2 tablespoons chili powder

1 teaspoon ground cumin

1/2 teaspoon salt

1/4 teaspoon black pepper

Instructions:

In a large skillet over medium heat, cook the ground beef until it is browned and crumbled. Drain any excess fat.

Transfer the ground beef to a crockpot. Add the onion, garlic, carrots, celery, bell pepper, beef broth, kidney beans, diced tomatoes, tomato paste, chili powder, cumin, salt, and pepper to the crockpot. Stir everything together.

Cover the crockpot and cook the chili on low heat for 8-10 hours, or on high heat for 4-5 hours.

Serve the chili hot, with your favorite toppings (such as grated cheese, diced onions, and sour cream).

Lasagna

Ingredients:

1 pound ground beef

1 large onion, diced

2 cloves garlic, minced

1 (24-ounce) jar spaghetti sauce

1 cup water

1 teaspoon dried oregano

1/2 teaspoon salt

1/4 teaspoon black pepper

9 lasagna noodles

1 cup ricotta cheese

1 cup grated mozzarella cheese

1/4 cup grated Parmesan cheese

Instructions:

In a large skillet over medium heat, cook the ground beef until it is browned and crumbled. Drain any excess fat. Transfer the ground beef to a crockpot.

Add the onion, garlic, spaghetti sauce, water, oregano, salt, and pepper to the crockpot. Stir everything together.

Break the lasagna noodles into pieces and add them to the crockpot, pushing them down into the sauce.

Cover the crockpot and cook the lasagna on low heat for 6-8 hours, or on high heat for 3-4 hours. About 30 minutes before the lasagna is done cooking, stir in the ricotta cheese.

Sprinkle the mozzarella cheese and Parmesan cheese over the top of the lasagna. Cover the crockpot and cook the lasagna for an additional 15-20 minutes, until the cheese is melted and bubbly.

Serve the lasagna hot, with your favorite sides.

My Crockpot Recipes

Lasagna

Classic Meat Lasagna

Ingredients:

1 pound ground beef

1 large onion, diced

2 cloves garlic, minced

1 (24-ounce) jar spaghetti sauce

1 (14.5-ounce) can diced tomatoes

1 teaspoon dried oregano

1/2 teaspoon salt

1/4 teaspoon black pepper

9 lasagna noodles

1 cup ricotta cheese

1 cup grated mozzarella cheese

1/4 cup grated Parmesan cheese

Instructions:

Preheat your oven to 350°F (180°C).

In a large skillet over medium heat, cook the ground beef until it is browned and crumbled. Drain any excess fat.

In a large bowl, mix together the cooked ground beef, onion, garlic, spaghetti sauce, diced tomatoes, oregano, salt, and pepper.

Spread a layer of the meat sauce in the bottom of a 9x13-inch baking dish. Top the sauce with a layer of lasagna noodles, breaking the noodles as needed to fit the dish. Spread a layer of the ricotta cheese over the noodles. Repeat the layers of sauce, noodles, and ricotta cheese until you have used up all of the ingredients, ending with a layer of sauce. Sprinkle the mozzarella cheese and Parmesan cheese over the top of the lasagna.

Cover the baking dish with aluminum foil. Bake the lasagna for 45 minutes. Remove the foil and continue baking the lasagna for an additional 15 minutes, until the cheese is melted and bubbly. Let the lasagna cool for a few minutes before slicing and serving.

Vegetable Lasagna

Ingredients:

1 large eggplant, cut into 1/4-inch slices

1 large zucchini, cut into 1/4-inch slices

1 large yellow squash, cut into 1/4-inch slices

1 large bell pepper, cut into 1/4-inch slices

1 large onion, cut into 1/4-inch slices

2 tablespoons olive oil

1/2 teaspoon salt

1/4 teaspoon black pepper

1 (24-ounce) jar spaghetti sauce

9 lasagna noodles

1 cup ricotta cheese

1 cup grated mozzarella cheese

1/4 cup grated Parmesan cheese

Instructions:

Preheat your oven to 400°F (200°C).

In a large bowl, toss the eggplant, zucchini, squash, bell pepper, and onion with the olive oil, salt, and pepper.

Spread the vegetables out in a single layer on a large baking sheet. Roast the vegetables for 20-25 minutes, until they are tender and slightly browned.

Reduce the oven temperature to 350°F (180°C).

In a large bowl, mix together the roasted vegetables and the spaghetti sauce.

Spread a layer of the vegetable sauce in the bottom of a 9 x13 inch baking dish. Top the sauce with a layer of lasagna noodles, breaking the noodles as needed to fit the dish. Spread a layer of the ricotta cheese over the noodles.

Continued...

Repeat the layers of sauce, noodles, and ricotta cheese until you have used up all of the ingredients, ending with a layer of sauce. Sprinkle the mozzarella cheese and Parmesan cheese over the top of the lasagna.

Cover the baking dish with aluminum foil. Bake the lasagna for 45 minutes. Remove the foil and continue baking the lasagna for an additional 15 minutes, until the cheese is melted and bubbly.

Let the lasagna cool for a few minutes before slicing and serving.

Spinach and Artichoke Lasagna

Ingredients:

2 (10-ounce) packages frozen chopped spinach, thawed and squeezed dry

1 (14-ounce) can artichoke hearts, drained and chopped

1 cup ricotta cheese

1/2 cup grated Parmesan cheese

1/2 cup grated mozzarella cheese

1 large egg, beaten

1/2 teaspoon salt

1/4 teaspoon black pepper

1 (24-ounce) jar spaghetti sauce

9 lasagna noodles

Instructions:

Preheat your oven to 350°F (180°C).

In a large bowl, mix together the spinach, artichoke hearts, ricotta cheese, Parmesan cheese, mozzarella cheese, egg, salt, and pepper.

Continued...

Spread a layer of the spaghetti sauce in the bottom of a 9x13-inch baking dish. Top the sauce with a layer of lasagna noodles, breaking the noodles as needed to fit the dish. Spread a layer of the spinach mixture over the noodles. Repeat the layers of sauce, noodles, and spinach mixture until you have used up all of the ingredients, ending with a layer of sauce.

Cover the baking dish with aluminum foil. Bake the lasagna for 45 minutes. Remove the foil and continue baking the lasagna for an additional 15 minutes, until the cheese is melted and bubbly.

Let the lasagna cool for a few minutes before slicing and serving.

Sausage and Mushroom Lasagna

Ingredients:

1 pound Italian sausage

1 large onion, diced

2 cloves garlic, minced

8 ounces mushrooms, sliced

1 (24-ounce) jar spaghetti sauce

1 (14.5-ounce) can diced tomatoes

1 teaspoon dried oregano

1/2 teaspoon salt

1/4 teaspoon black pepper

9 lasagna noodles

1 cup ricotta cheese

1 cup grated mozzarella cheese

1/4 cup grated Parmesan cheese

Continued...

Instructions:

Preheat your oven to 350°F (180°C).

In a large skillet over medium heat, cook the Italian sausage until it is browned and crumbled. Drain any excess fat.

Add the onion, garlic, and mushrooms to the skillet and cook for an additional 5-7 minutes, until the vegetables are tender. Stir in the spaghetti sauce, diced tomatoes, oregano, salt, and pepper.

Spread a layer of the sausage mixture in the bottom of a 9x13-inch baking dish. Top the sauce with a layer of lasagna noodles, breaking the noodles as needed to fit the dish. Spread a layer of the ricotta cheese over the noodles. Repeat the layers of sauce, noodles, and ricotta cheese until you have used up all of the ingredients, ending with a layer of sauce. Sprinkle the mozzarella cheese and Parmesan cheese over the top of the lasagna.

Cover the baking dish with aluminum foil. Bake the lasagna for 45 minutes. Remove the foil and continue baking the lasagna for an additional 15 minutes, until the cheese is melted and bubbly.

Let the lasagna cool for a few minutes before slicing and serving.

Pesto Lasagna

Ingredients:

1 cup basil pesto

1 cup ricotta cheese

1 cup grated mozzarella cheese

1/4 cup grated Parmesan cheese

1 (24-ounce) jar spaghetti sauce

9 lasagna noodles

Instructions:

Preheat your oven to 350°F (180°C).

In a small bowl, mix together the pesto and the ricotta cheese.

Spread a layer of the spaghetti sauce in the bottom of a 9x13-inch baking dish. Top the sauce with a layer of lasagna noodles, breaking the noodles as needed to fit the dish. Spread a layer of the pesto mixture over the noodles. Repeat the layers of sauce, noodles, and pesto mixture until you have used up all of the ingredients, ending with a layer of sauce.

Sprinkle the mozzarella cheese and Parmesan cheese over the top of the lasagna.

Cover the baking dish with aluminum foil. Bake the lasagna for 45 minutes.

Remove the foil and continue baking the lasagna for an additional 15 minutes, until the cheese is melted and bubbly.

Let the lasagna cool for a few minutes before slicing and serving.

My Lasagna Recipes

Simple Desserts

Chocolate Chip Cookies

Ingredients:

1 cup unsalted butter, softened

1 cup granulated sugar

1 cup light brown sugar

2 large eggs

1 teaspoon vanilla extract

2 1/2 cups all-purpose flour

1 teaspoon baking soda

1 teaspoon salt

1 cup semisweet chocolate chips

Instructions:

Preheat your oven to 350°F (180°C). Line a baking sheet with parchment paper.

In a large bowl, beat the butter, granulated sugar, and brown sugar together until the mixture is smooth and creamy. Beat in the eggs and vanilla extract.

In a medium bowl, whisk together the flour, baking soda, and salt. Gradually add the dry ingredients to the butter mixture, stirring until the dough comes together. Stir in the chocolate chips.

Drop spoonfuls of the dough onto the prepared baking sheet, spacing them about 2 inches apart.

Bake the cookies for 8-10 minutes, until they are lightly golden around the edges. Remove the cookies from the oven and let them cool on the baking sheet for a few minutes before transferring them to a wire rack to cool completely.

Banana Bread

Ingredients:

3 cups all-purpose flour

1 teaspoon baking soda

1/2 teaspoon salt

1 cup unsalted butter, softened

2 cups granulated sugar

4 large eggs

1 teaspoon vanilla extract

4 ripe bananas, mashed

Instructions:

Preheat your oven to 350°F (180°C). Grease a 9x5-inch loaf pan.

In a medium bowl, whisk together the flour, baking soda, and salt.

In a large bowl, beat the butter and sugar together until the mixture is light and fluffy. Beat in the eggs, one at a time, followed by the vanilla extract. Stir in the mashed bananas.

Gradually add the dry ingredients to the wet ingredients, stirring until the batter comes together. Pour the batter into the prepared loaf pan.

Bake the banana bread for 60-70 minutes, until a toothpick inserted into the center comes out clean. Let the banana bread cool in the pan for a few minutes before transferring it to a wire rack to cool completely.

Brownies

Ingredients:

1 cup unsalted butter, melted

2 cups granulated sugar

4 large eggs

1 cup all-purpose flour

1 cup unsweetened cocoa powder

1 teaspoon salt

Instructions:

Preheat your oven to 350°F (180°C). Grease a 9x13-inch baking dish.

In a large bowl, whisk together the melted butter and sugar. Whisk in the eggs, one at a time.

In a medium bowl, whisk together the flour, cocoa powder, and salt. Gradually add the dry ingredients to the wet ingredients, stirring until the batter is smooth and well-combined. Pour the batter into the prepared baking dish.

Bake the brownies for 25-30 minutes, until a toothpick inserted into the center comes out with a few moist crumbs attached.

Let the brownies cool in the pan for a few minutes before cutting them into squares and serving.

Chocolate Mousse

Ingredients:

8 ounces semisweet chocolate, chopped

1 cup heavy cream

2 large eggs, separated

2 tablespoons granulated sugar

1 teaspoon vanilla extract

Instructions:

Place the chocolate in a medium heatproof bowl. In a small saucepan, bring the cream to a boil over medium heat. Pour the hot cream over the chocolate and let it sit for a few minutes to melt the chocolate. Stir the mixture until it is smooth and well-combined.

In a large bowl, beat the egg whites with an electric mixer until they form soft peaks. Gradually add the sugar, continuing to beat the egg whites until they are stiff and glossy.

In a separate large bowl, beat the egg yolks until they are light and fluffy. Stir the egg yolks into the chocolate mixture. Gently fold in the whipped egg whites, followed by the vanilla extract.

Divide the mousse among individual serving dishes. Cover the dishes and refrigerate the mousse for at least 2 hours, or until it is firm. Serve the mousse chilled.

Cheesecake

Ingredients:

2 cups graham cracker crumbs

1/2 cup unsalted butter, melted

16 ounces cream cheese, softened

1 cup granulated sugar

2 large eggs

1 cup sour cream

1 tablespoon all-purpose flour

1 teaspoon vanilla extract

Instructions:

Preheat your oven to 350°F (180°C). Grease a 9-inch springform pan.

In a medium bowl, mix together the graham cracker crumbs and melted butter. Press the mixture into the bottom of the prepared pan.

In a large bowl, beat the cream cheese and sugar together until the mixture is smooth and creamy. Beat in the eggs, one at a time. Stir in the sour cream, flour, and vanilla extract.

Pour the cheesecake filling over the graham cracker crust. Smooth the top of the filling with a spatula.

Bake the cheesecake for 45-50 minutes, until it is set around the edges but still slightly jiggly in the center. Turn off the oven and let the cheesecake cool in the oven with the door closed for 1 hour. Remove the cheesecake from the oven and let it cool to room temperature. Cover the cheesecake and refrigerate it for at least 4 hours, or overnight.

Serve the cheesecake chilled, with your favorite toppings (such as whipped cream, fresh fruit, or chocolate sauce).

Apple Pie

Ingredients:

2 cups all-purpose flour

1 teaspoon salt

1 teaspoon sugar

1 cup unsalted butter, chilled and diced

1/2 cup ice water

6 cups thinly sliced apples

1/2 cup granulated sugar

1 tablespoon lemon juice

1 teaspoon cinnamon

1/4 teaspoon nutmeg

1 tablespoon unsalted butter

1 egg, beaten

Instructions:

In a large bowl, whisk together the flour, salt, and sugar. Cut in the butter with a pastry cutter or your fingers until the mixture resembles coarse sand. Gradually add the ice water, stirring until the dough comes together. Divide the dough in half and wrap each half in plastic wrap. Refrigerate the dough for at least 1 hour, or up to 2 days.

Preheat your oven to 375°F (190°C).

In a large bowl, toss together the apples, sugar, lemon juice, cinnamon, and nutmeg.

On a lightly floured surface, roll out one of the dough halves into a 12-inch circle. Transfer the dough to a 9-inch pie dish. Fill the pie dish with the apple mixture. Dot the top of the apples with the butter.

Continued...

Roll out the remaining dough half into a 12-inch circle. Cut the dough into strips and lay them over the top of the pie in a lattice pattern. Brush the top of the pie with the beaten egg.

Bake the pie for 45-50 minutes, until the crust is golden brown and the filling is bubbly. Let the pie cool to room temperature before serving.

Strawberry Shortcake

Ingredients:

2 cups all-purpose flour

1 tablespoon baking powder

1/2 teaspoon salt

6 tablespoons unsalted butter, chilled and diced

3/4 cup milk

2 cups sliced strawberries

1/4 cup granulated sugar

1 cup heavy cream

1 teaspoon vanilla extract

Instructions:

Preheat your oven to 425°F (220°C). Line a baking sheet with parchment paper.

In a large bowl, whisk together the flour, baking powder, and salt. Cut in the butter with a pastry cutter or your fingers until the mixture resembles coarse sand. Gradually add the milk, stirring until the dough comes together.

Continued...

Drop spoonfuls of the dough onto the prepared baking sheet, spacing them about 2 inches apart. Bake the shortcakes for 10-12 minutes, until they are golden brown. Remove the shortcakes from the oven and let them cool on the baking sheet for a few minutes before transferring them to a wire rack to cool completely.

In a medium bowl, toss together the strawberries and sugar. Let the mixture sit for 15-20 minutes, until the strawberries release their juices.

In a large bowl, beat the heavy cream and vanilla extract with an electric mixer until stiff peaks form.

To assemble the strawberry shortcake, split a shortcake in half horizontally.

Place the bottom half on a plate and top it with a spoonful of the strawberry mixture. Add a dollop of whipped cream on top of the strawberries.

Place the top half of the shortcake on top of the whipped cream. Repeat with the remaining shortcakes.

Serve the strawberry shortcakes immediately.

Chocolate Pudding

Ingredients:

1/2 cup granulated sugar

1/3 cup unsweetened cocoa powder

1/4 cup cornstarch

1/4 teaspoon salt

2 3/4 cups milk

3 ounces semisweet chocolate, chopped

1 teaspoon vanilla extract

Instructions:

In a medium saucepan, whisk together the sugar, cocoa powder, cornstarch, and salt. Gradually add the milk, whisking until the mixture is smooth.

Place the saucepan over medium heat and cook the pudding, stirring constantly, until it comes to a boil. Reduce the heat to low and continue cooking the pudding for an additional 2 minutes, until it is thick and creamy.

Remove the saucepan from the heat and stir in the chocolate and vanilla extract until the chocolate is melted.

Pour the pudding into individual serving dishes. Cover the dishes and refrigerate the pudding for at least 2 hours, or until it is chilled.

Serve the chocolate pudding chilled.

Fruit Tart

Ingredients:

1 cup all-purpose flour

1/2 cup unsalted butter, chilled and diced

1/4 cup granulated sugar

1 large egg yolk

1 teaspoon vanilla extract

4 cups mixed fruit (such as berries, kiwi, and sliced mango)

1/2 cup apricot jam

Instructions:

Preheat your oven to 350°F (180°C). Grease a 9-inch tart pan with a removable bottom.

In a large bowl, mix together the flour, butter, and sugar with a pastry cutter or your fingers until the mixture resembles coarse sand. Stir in the egg yolk and vanilla extract until the dough comes together. Press the dough into the bottom and up the sides of the prepared tart pan.

Bake the tart shell for 15-20 minutes, until it is lightly golden around the edges. Remove the tart shell from the oven and let it cool completely.

In a small saucepan, melt the apricot jam over low heat. Brush the jam over the bottom of the cooled tart shell.

Arrange the fruit over the top of the jam in a decorative pattern. Serve the tart immediately, or refrigerate it until you are ready to serve it.

Chocolate Fondue

Ingredients:

12 ounces semisweet chocolate, chopped

1 cup heavy cream

2 tablespoons unsalted butter

Assorted fruit, cookies, and other dipping items (such as marshmallows, pretzel rods, and graham crackers)

Instructions:

In a medium saucepan, combine the chocolate, cream, and butter. Place the saucepan over medium heat and cook the mixture, stirring constantly, until the chocolate is melted and the fondue is smooth and well-combined.

Transfer the fondue to a fondue pot or a small slow cooker set to the "low" setting. Serve the fondue immediately, with the dipping items on the side.

My Dessert Recipes

Punches

Sparkling Berry Punch

In a punch bowl, combine 1 liter of chilled sparkling water, 1 cup of frozen mixed berries (such as raspberries, blackberries, and blueberries), 1/2 cup of raspberry sorbet, and 1/4 cup of lemon juice.

Stir well to combine the ingredients.

Serve the punch over ice, with a few berries and a slice of lemon as a garnish, if desired.

Tropical Punch

In a punch bowl, mix together 1 liter of pineapple juice, 1 liter of orange juice, and 1 liter of lemon-lime soda.

Stir in 1 cup of diced mango, 1 cup of diced pineapple, and 1/2 cup of maraschino cherries.

Serve the punch over ice, with a few slices of mango or pineapple as a garnish, if desired.

Cherry Limeade Punch

In a punch bowl, mix together 1 liter of cherry limeade, 1 liter of lemon-lime soda, and 1 cup of maraschino cherry juice.

Stir in 1 cup of frozen cherries and 1/2 cup of lime slices.

Serve the punch over ice, with a few cherries and a slice of lime as a garnish, if desired.

Raspberry Lemonade Punch

In a punch bowl, mix together 1 liter of raspberry lemonade, 1 liter of lemon-lime soda, and 1 cup of frozen raspberries.

Stir in 1/2 cup of lemon slices and 1/4 cup of sugar.

Serve the punch over ice, with a few raspberries and a slice of lemon as a garnish, if desired.

Ginger Peach Punch

In a punch bowl, combine 1 liter of ginger ale, 1 liter of peach nectar, and 1 cup of frozen peaches.

Stir in 1/2 cup of peeled and diced ginger and 1/4 cup of lemon juice.

Serve the punch over ice, with a few slices of peach and a slice of lemon as a garnish, if desired.

My Punch (and drinks) Recipes

Simple to Make Candies

Homemade Fudge

Line an 8x8-inch square pan with parchment paper.

In a medium saucepan, combine 1 cup of heavy cream, 1 cup of sugar, 4 tablespoons of unsalted butter, and a pinch of salt.

Heat the mixture over medium heat, stirring constantly, until the sugar has dissolved and the mixture comes to a boil.

Reduce the heat to low and simmer for about 5 minutes, until the mixture reaches the soft ball stage (235-240°F on a candy thermometer).

Remove the saucepan from the heat and stir in 1 cup of semisweet chocolate chips and 1 teaspoon of vanilla extract until the chocolate is completely melted.

Pour the mixture into the prepared pan and let it cool completely.

Once cooled, cut the fudge into small squares and serve.

Chocolate Truffles

In a small saucepan, heat 1/2 cup of heavy cream over medium heat until it comes to a boil. Remove the saucepan from the heat and add 8 ounces of chopped semisweet chocolate.

Stir the chocolate until it is completely melted and the mixture is smooth.

Pour the mixture into a shallow dish and let it cool completely in the fridge.

Once cooled, use a small cookie scoop or spoon to form the mixture into small balls.

Roll the truffles in cocoa powder, powdered sugar, or your choice of coating (such as chopped nuts or sprinkles) to finish.

Peanut Butter Balls

In a medium bowl, mix together 1 cup of smooth peanut butter, 1/2 cup of powdered sugar, and 2 tablespoons of unsalted butter until well combined.

Use a small cookie scoop or spoon to form the mixture into small balls.

Roll the balls in powdered sugar and place them on a wax paper-lined baking sheet.

Chill the balls in the fridge for at least 30 minutes, until firm.

Once chilled, melt 8 ounces of semisweet chocolate in a small saucepan over low heat. Dip the peanut butter balls in the melted chocolate, using a toothpick to hold them, and place them back on the wax paper-lined baking sheet.

Let the chocolate harden before serving.

Chocolate-Covered Pretzels

Line a baking sheet with wax paper.

Melt 8 ounces of semisweet chocolate in a small saucepan over low heat.

Dip small pretzel twists or rods in the melted chocolate, using a toothpick to hold them, and place them on the wax paper-lined baking sheet.

Repeat with the remaining pretzels.

Let the chocolate harden before serving.

My Candy Recipes

Breakfasts That Are More Involved

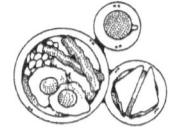

Quiche

Ingredients:

1 pie crust (homemade or store-bought)

4 eggs

1 cup milk

1/2 cup heavy cream

1/2 teaspoon salt

1/4 teaspoon black pepper

1 cup diced ham

1 cup grated cheese (such as cheddar or Swiss)

1/2 cup diced onion

1/2 cup diced bell pepper

Instructions:

Preheat your oven to 350°F (180°C).

Press the pie crust into a 9-inch pie dish, crimping the edges as desired.

In a large bowl, whisk together the eggs, milk, heavy cream, salt, and pepper. Stir in the diced ham, grated cheese, diced onion, and diced bell pepper.

Pour the egg mixture into the pie crust.

Bake the quiche for 45-50 minutes, until it is set and the top is golden brown. Let the quiche cool for a few minutes before slicing and serving.

Huevos Rancheros

Ingredients:

4 eggs

4 corn tortillas

1 cup salsa

1/2 cup grated cheese (such as cheddar or Monterey Jack)

1/4 cup diced red onion

1/4 cup diced cilantro

1/4 cup diced avocado

Instructions:

Heat a large skillet over medium heat. Crack the eggs into the skillet and let them cook for about 1-2 minutes, until the bottom starts to set. Use a spatula to gently stir the eggs, scraping the bottom and sides of the skillet as you go.

When the eggs are almost cooked to your desired level of doneness, add a spoonful of salsa over the top of each egg. Sprinkle a tablespoon of grated cheese over the salsa.

Place a corn tortilla on top of each egg. Cover the skillet and let everything cook for about 1-2 minutes, until the tortillas are hot and the cheese is melted.

To serve, top each huevos rancheros with diced red onion, diced cilantro, and diced avocado.

Breakfast Strata

Ingredients:

6 slices bread

6 eggs

1 cup milk

1/2 cup heavy cream

1/2 teaspoon salt

1/4 teaspoon black pepper

1 cup diced ham

1 cup grated cheese (such as cheddar or Swiss)

1/2 cup diced onion

1/2 cup diced bell pepper

Instructions:

Preheat your oven to 350°F (180°C).

Arrange the bread slices in the bottom of a 9x13-inch baking dish.

In a large bowl, whisk together the eggs, milk, heavy cream, salt, and pepper. Stir in the diced ham, grated cheese, diced onion, and diced bell pepper.

Pour the egg mixture over the bread slices in the baking dish.

Bake the strata for 45-50 minutes, until it is set and the top is golden brown. Let the strata cool for a few minutes before slicing and serving.

Breakfast Enchiladas

Ingredients:

8 eggs

1 cup milk

1/2 teaspoon salt

1/4 teaspoon black pepper

1 cup diced ham

1 cup grated cheese (such as cheddar or Monterey Jack)

1/2 cup diced onion

1/2 cup diced bell pepper

8 corn tortillas

1 cup salsa

1/2 cup grated cheese (such as cheddar or Monterey Jack)

1/4 cup diced red onion

1/4 cup diced cilantro

1/4 cup diced avocado

Instructions:

Preheat your oven to 350°F (180°C).

In a large bowl, whisk together the eggs, milk, salt, and pepper. Stir in the diced ham, grated cheese, diced onion, and diced bell pepper.

Spread about 1/4 cup of the egg mixture down the center of each corn tortilla. Roll the tortillas up tightly and place them seam-side down in a large, greased baking dish.

Pour the salsa over the top of the enchiladas. Sprinkle the grated cheese over the salsa.

Bake the enchiladas for 25-30 minutes, until they are hot and the cheese is melted and bubbly.

To serve, top the enchiladas with diced red onion, diced cilantro, and diced avocado.

Breakfast Sandwich

Ingredients:

4 eggs

4 slices bacon

4 English muffins

4 slices cheese (such as cheddar or American)

Lettuce, tomato, and mayonnaise, for serving (optional)

Instructions:

Heat a large skillet over medium heat. Add the eggs and let them cook for about 1-2 minutes, until the bottom starts to set. Use a spatula to gently stir the eggs, scraping the bottom and sides of the skillet as you go.

When the eggs are almost cooked to your desired level of doneness, place a slice of cheese on top of each egg. Cover the skillet and let everything cook for about 1 minute, until the cheese is melted.

Meanwhile, cook the bacon in a separate skillet until it is crispy.

Toast the English muffins until they are warm and slightly crispy.

To assemble the sandwiches, place a slice of cheese-topped eggs on the bottom half of each English muffin.

Top the eggs with a slice of bacon, lettuce, tomato, and mayonnaise (if using).

Cover with the top half of the English muffins.

Serve the breakfast sandwiches hot.

My More Involved Breakfast Recipes

Coffee!

Iced Coffee

Brew a strong pot of coffee, using your preferred method. Pour the coffee into a pitcher and let it cool to room temperature.

Once cooled, add in some milk, sweetened condensed milk, or your preferred sweetener to taste. Stir well to combine.

Pour the iced coffee over ice and serve. You can also add a few coffee ice cubes to keep the drink from getting watered down as the ice melts.

Mocha Frappuccino

In a blender, combine 1 cup of cold coffee, 1 cup of milk, 2 tablespoons of chocolate syrup, 2 tablespoons of sugar, and a handful of ice.

Blend the ingredients until smooth.

Pour the frappuccino into a tall glass and top with whipped cream and a drizzle of chocolate syrup, if desired.

Coffee Smoothie

In a blender, combine 1 cup of cold coffee, 1 banana, 1 cup of frozen berries, 1 cup of Greek yogurt, and 1 tablespoon of honey.

Blend the ingredients until smooth.

Pour the smoothie into a tall glass and serve.

Coffee-Rubbed Steak

In a small bowl, mix together 2 tablespoons of finely ground coffee, 1 tablespoon of paprika, 1 tablespoon of brown sugar, 1 teaspoon of garlic powder, 1 teaspoon of onion powder, 1/2 teaspoon of cumin, and 1/2 teaspoon of salt.

Rub the mixture all over a steak of your choice and let it marinate in the fridge for at least 1 hour (or up to 24 hours).

Preheat a grill or broiler to high heat.

Grill or broil the steak for about 4-5 minutes per side, or until it reaches your desired level of doneness.

Let the steak rest for a few minutes before slicing and serving.

Coffee-Flavored Ice Cream

In a medium saucepan, combine 2 cups of heavy cream, 1 cup of whole milk, 3/4 cup of sugar, and 2 tablespoons of finely ground coffee. Heat the mixture over medium heat, stirring constantly, until the sugar has dissolved.

Remove the saucepan from the heat and stir in 1 teaspoon of vanilla extract.

Pour the mixture into a large bowl and let it cool to room temperature.

Once cooled, cover the bowl with plastic wrap and chill it in the fridge for at least 2 hours (or up to 24 hours). Once chilled, churn the mixture in an ice cream maker according to the manufacturer's instructions.

Transfer the ice cream to a container and freeze it until firm, about 2 hours.

Serve the ice cream topped with a drizzle of chocolate sauce or chopped nuts, if desired.

My Coffee Recipes

Potatoes

Roasted Potatoes

Preheat your oven to 400°F.

Wash and cut your potatoes into wedges or small cubes. You can leave the skin on or peel it off, depending on your preference.

Place the potatoes in a bowl and toss with enough olive oil to coat them evenly. Add in any seasonings you like – some good options include rosemary, garlic, paprika, and thyme.

Spread the potatoes out on a baking sheet in a single layer.

Roast the potatoes for 20-30 minutes, or until they are tender and golden brown. Flip them once or twice during cooking to ensure even browning.

Serve the roasted potatoes hot, garnished with additional seasonings if desired.

Mashed Potatoes

Wash and chop your potatoes into 1-inch cubes. Place the potatoes in a large pot and cover with cold water. Add a pinch of salt to the water.

Bring the water to a boil over high heat, then reduce the heat to medium-low and simmer until the potatoes are tender when pierced with a fork, about 10-15 minutes.

Drain the potatoes and return them to the pot. Add in a few tablespoons of butter and enough milk to make the potatoes creamy. Mash the potatoes with a potato masher or a fork until they reach your desired consistency.

Season the mashed potatoes with salt to taste. You can also add in any other ingredients you like, such as shredded cheese, roasted garlic, or caramelized onions.

Serve the mashed potatoes hot, garnished with additional butter or cheese if desired.

Grilled Potatoes

Preheat your grill to medium heat.

Wash and slice your potatoes into thin rounds, about 1/4 inch thick. Place the potato slices in a bowl and toss with enough olive oil to coat them evenly. Add in a pinch of salt and any other seasonings you like – some good options include garlic, paprika, and thyme.

Arrange the potato slices on the grill in a single layer. Grill the potatoes for 5-7 minutes on each side, or until they are tender and lightly charred.

Serve the grilled potatoes hot, garnished with additional seasonings if desired.

Twice-baked Potatoes

Preheat your oven to 400°F.

Wash and prick your potatoes with a fork a few times. Place the potatoes on a baking sheet and bake for 45-60 minutes, or until they are tender when pierced with a fork.

Let the potatoes cool until they are cool enough to handle. Cut each potato in half lengthwise and scoop out the insides, leaving a thin layer of potato attached to the skin.

Place the potato insides in a bowl and mash them with a fork or potato masher. Add in a few tablespoons of butter and enough milk to make the potatoes creamy. Stir in any additional toppings you like, such as shredded cheese, bacon, and green onions.

Spoon the potato mixture back into the potato skins. Place the potatoes back on the baking sheet and bake for an additional 10-15 minutes, or until the tops are golden and bubbly.

Serve the twice-baked potatoes hot, garnished with additional toppings if desired.

Potato Salad

Wash and chop your potatoes into 1-inch cubes. Place the potatoes in a large pot and cover with cold water. Add a pinch of salt to the water.

Bring the water to a boil over high heat, then reduce the heat to medium-low and simmer until the potatoes are tender when pierced with a fork, about 10-15 minutes.

Drain the potatoes and let them cool until they are cool enough to handle.

Chop the cooled potatoes into small pieces and place them in a large bowl.

In a separate small bowl, mix together mayonnaise, diced onions, and any other seasonings you like (such as mustard, dill, and celery seed). Pour the mayonnaise mixture over the potatoes and toss to coat.

Cover the bowl with plastic wrap and refrigerate the potato salad until chilled, at least 1 hour.

Serve the potato salad chilled or at room temperature, garnished with additional diced onions or herbs if desired.

My Potato Recipes

Gravy

Basic Meat Gravy

This gravy is made from the drippings of roast beef, pork, or lamb, and is a classic accompaniment to roast meats.

To make it, first, skim the fat off the drippings in the roasting pan, and then add enough beef broth to the pan to measure about 2 cups. Bring the mixture to a boil, and then whisk in 2 tablespoons of cornstarch that has been mixed with 2 tablespoons of cold water. Cook the gravy, stirring constantly, until it thickens and comes to a boil.

Season to taste with salt and pepper.

Mushroom Gravy

This gravy is a delicious accompaniment to roast chicken or turkey, and is made by sautéing sliced mushrooms in butter until they are browned.

Then, whisk in some all-purpose flour and cook for a few minutes, until the flour is lightly browned. Slowly whisk in chicken broth and bring the mixture to a boil, whisking constantly. Reduce the heat to a simmer and let the gravy cook for about 10 minutes, or until it has thickened.

Season to taste with salt and pepper.

Onion Gravy

This gravy is a great accompaniment to roast beef or pork, and is made by slowly caramelizing sliced onions in butter until they are deeply browned.

Then, whisk in some all-purpose flour and cook for a few minutes, until the flour is lightly browned. Slowly whisk in beef broth and bring the mixture to a boil, whisking constantly.

Reduce the heat to a simmer and let the gravy cook for about 10 minutes, or until it has thickened.

Season to taste with salt and pepper.

Biscuit Gravy

This creamy, southern-style gravy is made with sausage, flour, milk, and biscuits.

To make it, cook crumbled sausage in a pan until it is browned, and then whisk in some all-purpose flour. Cook the flour for a few minutes, until it is lightly browned, and then slowly whisk in milk. Bring the mixture to a boil, and then reduce the heat to a simmer. Let the gravy cook for about 10 minutes, or until it has thickened.

Season to taste with salt and pepper. Serve the gravy over warm biscuits.

Gravy made from Pan Drippings

This gravy is a quick and easy way to make a flavorful sauce using the drippings from a roast chicken or turkey.

To make it, first, skim the fat off the drippings in the roasting pan, and then add enough chicken broth to the pan to measure about 2 cups. Bring the mixture to a boil, and then whisk in 2 tablespoons of cornstarch that has been mixed with 2 tablespoons of cold water.

Cook the gravy, stirring constantly, until it thickens and comes to a boil.

Season to taste with salt and pepper.

Chocolate Gravy

Ingredients:

1 cup all-purpose flour

1 cup granulated sugar

1/4 cup unsweetened cocoa powder

1/4 teaspoon salt

3 cups whole milk

Instructions:

In a medium saucepan, whisk together the flour, sugar, cocoa powder, and salt. Slowly whisk in the milk, making sure to get rid of any lumps.

Place the saucepan over medium heat and cook, whisking constantly, until the mixture comes to a boil and thickens.

Reduce the heat to low and let the gravy simmer for an additional 2-3 minutes, or until it reaches your desired thickness.

Serve the chocolate gravy hot, over warm biscuits.

My Gravy Recipes

Pizza

Margherita Pizza

Spread tomato sauce over a prepared pizza crust, top with slices of fresh mozzarella and torn basil leaves, and bake until the cheese is melted and bubbly.

Pepperoni Pizza

Spread tomato sauce over a prepared pizza crust and top with sliced pepperoni and grated mozzarella cheese. Bake until the cheese is melted and bubbly.

Salami may be substituted for pepperoni.

BBQ Chicken Pizza

Spread BBQ sauce over a prepared pizza crust and top with diced cooked chicken, red onions, and cheddar cheese. Bake until the cheese is melted and bubbly.

Hawaiian Pizza

Spread tomato sauce over a prepared pizza crust and top with sliced ham, pineapple chunks, and grated mozzarella cheese. Bake until the cheese is melted and bubbly.

Veggie Pizza

Spread tomato sauce over a prepared pizza crust and top with your favorite vegetables, such as bell peppers, mushrooms, and olives. Sprinkle with grated mozzarella cheese and bake until the cheese is melted and bubbly.

Pizza Crust

Ingredients

1 cup warm water (110 degrees F)

2 1/4 teaspoons active dry yeast

3 1/2 cups all-purpose flour

2 tablespoons olive oil

1 teaspoon salt

Directions:

In a large bowl, combine the water and yeast. Let stand for 5 minutes, until the yeast is foamy.

Add the flour, olive oil, and salt to the bowl with the yeast mixture. Stir until a dough forms.

Turn the dough out onto a lightly floured surface and knead for about 5 minutes, until it is smooth and elastic.

Place the dough in a greased bowl, cover with a damp cloth, and set aside in a warm place to rise until doubled in size, about 1 hour.

Preheat the oven to 425 degrees F.

Punch down the dough and roll it out on a lightly floured surface to the desired size. Transfer the dough to a baking sheet or pizza pan.

Top the dough with your desired toppings and bake for 15-20 minutes, until the crust is golden brown.

My Pizza Recipes

The team at OffBeatReads hopes that you will enjoy this collection of recipes for years to come!
For more great books of all genres, including *Adventures to Go*, check out:
OffBeatReads.com

www.ingramcontent.com/pod-product-compliance
Lightning Source LLC
Chambersburg PA
CBHW030153100526
44592CB00009B/248